Date Night

NEW YORK
CITY

Date Night: New York City

13-Digit ISBN: 978-1-64643-356-8
10-Digit ISBN: 1-64643-356-4

This book may be ordered by mail from the publisher. Please include $5.99 for postage and handling. Please support your local bookseller first!

Books published by Cider Mill Press Book Publishers are available at special discounts for bulk purchases in the United States by corporations, institutions, and other organizations. For more information, please contact the publisher.

Cider Mill Press Book Publishers
"Where good books are ready for press"
501 Nelson Place
Nashville, Tennessee 37214

cidermillpress.com

Typography: GarageGothic, LiebeLotte, Sofia Pro

All vectors and images used under official license from Shutterstock.com.

Printed in Malaysia

23 24 25 26 27 OFF 5 4 3 2 1
First Edition

Date Night

NEW YORK CITY

**50 Creative, Budget-Friendly Dates
for the City That Never Sleeps**

CHLOE DICKENSON

CIDER MILL
PRESS

BOOK
PUBLISHERS

CONTENTS

INTRODUCTION

Paris, Venice, and Rome might be more synonymous with the idea of romance, but their American sister, New York City, also deserves recognition as one of the most romantic cities in the world.

The allure of the Big Apple beckons millions of couples into its heart every single year. With its breathtaking sunsets over the Hudson River, the dazzling lights of skyscrapers twinkling at night, and the abundance of intimate restaurants that open their doors every evening, New York City is the epitome of romance.

Dating has always been prevalent in New York City, especially since it came to the forefront of every twenty-something's mind in the nineties thanks to TV shows such as *Sex and the City*. The likes of Samantha, Carrie, Miranda, and Charlotte showed people all over the world that New York City is the place to be when it comes to love, and from then on the City That Never Sleeps has invited romantics from all over the world into its midst.

New York City is a beacon for many things, and romance is arguably one of its most defining traits. Cozy cafés in the East Village provide the perfect backdrop for a first-date coffee meetup, whereas the towering heights of the city's most famous observation decks offer a swoon-worthy Hollywood movie setting that would have even the most unromantic souls feeling like they've won the love lottery.

A stroll along the iconic Brooklyn Bridge might seem like an archetypal New York tourist activity, but its romantic association is not to be ignored. In fact, there are many romantic locations you might have overlooked that make for quintessential meeting places for lovers. Disney film *Enchanted* chose New York City as its setting, and if it's good enough for an animated Disney princess who's come to life, it's good enough to host many a date night.

It's also a food lover's paradise. With almost 30,000 restaurants across the five boroughs, dining and dating in NYC is remarkably easy. Alongside

Home to picturesque sunset spots, gorgeous parks, wonderful restaurants, and a smorgasbord of remarkable date opportunities, New York City is a dream location for a first or fiftieth date.

dozens of Michelin-star restaurants, highly coveted eateries, and world-class dining experiences, New York is proud to boast some incredible places to eat. A New

York brunch cruise along the East River and Hudson River, for instance, provides one of the most remarkable settings for brunch in the city. With views of the Statue of Liberty while you cruise and delightful delicacies to be enjoyed, there are very few people who could resist the opportunity to embark on a brunch cruise in one of the most romantic cities in the world.

Those who would prefer to avoid the water and reach thrilling heights instead will take solace in one of New York's many rooftop bars. 230 Fifth is one of the most sought-after rooftop bars in Manhattan, providing dramatic views of the Empire State Building and bottomless brunch events that combine limitless drinks with delectable dishes.

Couples seeking the opportunity to relax while on a date in the city will find countless things to do to satisfy their de-stressing needs. An afternoon at the Couple Spa is undoubtedly one of the most romantic things to enjoy in New York City, and with world-class treatments and exclusive packages, this celebrity-loved spa located in the exclusive Upper East Side is a surefire way to relax and rejuvenate.

Going on a date in New York City has never been easier thanks to the endless hotspots that provide idyllic locations for a nerve-wracking first date or a special 50th wedding anniversary.

Finding the perfect date idea in New York, however, can be a little overwhelming due to the enormity of the city, so this epic guide of the 50 best romantic date ideas for couples in New York City is the ultimate go-to pocket guide for lovers everywhere.

Central Park

OBSERVATION DECKS

Home to numerous observation decks—including the world-renowned Top of the Rock, the emblematic Empire State Building, and the recently opened Summit One Vanderbilt—there are plenty of opportunities for romance atop some of the city's tallest structures.

THE EMPIRE STATE BUILDING

The Empire State Building is unquestionably one of the most famous landmarks in the whole city, and movies such as *Sleepless in Seattle* and *King Kong* have turned the iconic skyscraper into a romantic touchstone.

There are two observation decks to be enjoyed: the first one is located on the 86th floor and tickets start at $44 for adults. The second observation deck resides on the 102nd floor, a whopping 1,250 feet above the sprawling streets of Midtown Manhattan. Rising 16 floors higher costs an additional $35 on top of the initial $44 entry ticket.

Have a sweet tooth? Just across the road from the Empire State Building, you'll find a Lindt Chocolate Shop whose walls are covered from floor to ceiling with a vast assortment of chocolate truffles. Pick up some

NOT TO MISS

The 102nd-floor obser-vation deck boasts breathtaking 360-degree views across the entire city. On the clearest days, you can see as far as 80 miles in every direction. For the ultimate romantic experience, it's worth going the extra mile (or extra 16 floors) to enjoy an unrivaled view that is sure to be remembered for years to come.

treats and walk the six blocks to Bryant Park where you can enjoy them in the sunshine.

EMPIRE STATE BUILDING:
20 W 34th Street, New York, NY 10001

BRYANT PARK:
Between 40th and 42nd Street and 5th and 6th Avenue, New York, NY 10018

TOP OF THE ROCK

The Top of the Rock is the best observation deck in Manhattan if you want to enjoy spectacular views of the Empire State Building.

From the open-air roof deck on the 70th floor, you can see the sprawling acres of Central Park on one side and the Empire State Building and Downtown Manhattan on the other. These 360-degree views are utterly breathtaking.

Tickets to visit the Top of the Rock start at $40 for adults for general admission and $50 for sunset tickets. There is no time limit on how long you can spend at the three observation decks, so it's a fantastic place to enjoy in the evening and into the night if you want to see the twinkling lights of the city from above after the sun has set.

The Top of the Rock observation deck resides in the Rockefeller Center, which is a commercial complex comprising 19 buildings across 22 acres in Midtown

NOT TO MISS

Planning your date to the Top of the Rock in time for sunset will undoubtedly be one of the most magical moments of your life. If you go on a clear day, the sunset in the city coats the buildings and skyscrapers in the most beautiful shades of orange and red. It's an experience that cannot be missed.

Manhattan. At the Rockefeller Center, you'll also find the Rink, which is home to the iconic ice skating rink in the winter months and the newly opened Flipper's Roller Boogie Palace in the summer—both of which make excellent additional places to go on a date after you've visited the observation deck.

THE TOP OF THE ROCK:

30 Rockefeller Plaza, New York, NY 10112

THE RINK AT THE ROCKEFELLER:

600 5th Avenue, Rockefeller Center, New York, NY 10020

SUMMIT ONE VANDERBILT

Summit One Vanderbilt is the newest observation deck in New York City. There are multiple viewing points throughout the building where you can enjoy exquisite, panoramic views of the city from 1,000 feet above the ground. Unlike the four other observation decks in the city, this one boasts an awesome array of immersive and interactive exhibits: Air, Levitation, Ascent, and Après.

Air is a display like no other: with floor-to-ceiling mirrors encompassing an entire room, the reflections of the surrounding city bounce off one another, creating an ethereal experience that's mind-blowingly awesome.

ROMANTIC DINING

The Oyster Bar located on the lower level of Grand Central serves a vast selection of 25 different types of fish and up to 30 varieties of oysters. Seafood is renowned for being one of the most romantic cuisines you can indulge in, so head for a decadent dining experience at The Oyster Bar inside one of the most famous train stations in the world.

The Levitation sky boxes let you stand inside glass boxes and view the bustling city streets below you in a view like no other.

Ascent is the world's largest exterior glass-floor elevator that takes you even further into the sky for transcendent views across Manhattan.

Once you've enjoyed the magic of the numerous rooms and exhibits, head to Après—Summit's very own open-air terrace and indoor lounge—where you can enjoy delicious delicacies and delightful drinks.

General admission tickets to Summit start at $42 for adults. You can upgrade to an Ascent ticket that includes the cost of riding in the glass elevator starting at $62, or purchase the Summit Signature Experience ticket for $56 which includes general admission and a signature cocktail at Après.

You gain access to Summit via the 42nd Street entrance of Grand Central Terminal, so you can also check out this romantic train station before or after your visit to the observation deck.

SUMMIT ONE VANDERBILT:
45 E 42nd Street, New York, NY 10017

GRAND CENTRAL OYSTER BAR:
89 E 42nd Street, Lower Level, New York, NY 10017

♥ Summit One Vanderbilt

EDGE

Located in Hudson Yards, Edge is the tallest outdoor observation deck in the Western Hemisphere, so you're guaranteed to experience dizzying heights and spectacular views with your partner.

The viewing platform has the illusion of being suspended in midair, and the mesmerizing views from the glass-bottomed deck 100 stories high are absolutely stunning. As it's located in Hudson Yards, you get a completely different vantage point than what the Midtown observation decks offer, which makes this an entirely unique date in New York City.

General admission tickets to visit the viewing platform start at $36 per person, and the City Climb tickets start at $185 per person.

LOOKING FOR A THRILL?

If you're interested in really spicing up your date at Edge, you can purchase additional tickets to City Climb, which is the highest open-air building ascent in the world. From here, you'll scale the outside of the building 1,200 feet above the ground, all while admiring the otherworldly views of the city from an incredible vantage point.

Once you've had your fill of the views, head to the champagne bar where you can sip on delicious bubbles and signature cocktails.

 EDGE:

30 Hudson Yards, New York, NY 10001

ONE WORLD OBSERVATORY

Residing in the Financial District of Manhattan, One World Trade Center is a building that can be seen from all over the city thanks to its symbolic height of 1,776 feet. As it's the tallest building in the Western Hemisphere, it provides the perfect vantage point for seeing New York City from above.

You'll ascend over 100 stories in just 47 seconds, so the elevator ride alone will be an experience to remember. Once you're at the top of the observation deck, unparalleled views await as you're treated to a panoramic perspective of the surrounding city skyline.

DINING HIGH ABOVE THE GROUND

Once you've checked out the views, head to ONE Dine on the 101st floor for a romantic meal in the sky—you can tuck into delectable dishes such as calamari, meatballs, swordfish, steak, and more.

This makes for a wonderful addition to your time at the observation deck, especially if you want to make your date extra special—it's not often that you get the chance to eat 101 floors above the ground!

Standard tickets start at $44 per person, making it one of the most expensive observation decks in New York City, but it's something that you're not likely to forget anytime soon.

ONE WORLD OBSERVATORY:

117 West Street, New York, NY 10007

IN THE PARKS

New York City is home to an abundance of wonderful outdoor spaces that are perfect for pitching a picnic, relaxing in the sunshine, or frolicking in the grass. Here are some of the most date-worthy parks in New York City.

CENTRAL PARK

Central Park is unquestionably the most emblematic park in New York City, and it's famous the world over for its sprawling 843 acres of grassland, lakes, bridges, and more.

One of the best activities to enjoy in Central Park is the Loeb Boathouse, from which you can hire boats in the summer for $20 per hour. Each boat can hold up to four people, but they're ideal for just two people enjoying a romantic row on the Lake. You can also eat at the Boathouse restaurant, where they serve delicious dishes such as roasted lamb, salmon, and crispy chicken. See page 104 for more details.

Central Park is also a wonderful place for a picnic, and thanks to the many delis, cafés, and food markets located near many of the entrances to the park, you're spoiled for choice when it comes to picking up picnic food. Levain Bakery has two branches on the Upper West Side, West 74th Street and Amsterdam Avenue, and they offer the most heavenly chocolate chip cookies for $4.50 each or $29 for a box of four.

For something more savory, head inside the Shops at Columbus Circle to Whole Foods Market, where you can pick up some gourmet sandwiches and an assortment of hot and cold dishes that make the perfect picnic pairing.

Fans of the Beatles will enjoy admiring Strawberry Fields: a tiled mosaic memorial dedicated to the late John Lennon. For true fairy-tale romance, head to Belvedere Castle in the heart of Central Park. This Gothic castle dates all the way back to 1869, and from its vantage point on top of Vista Rock, you can enjoy spectacular views across the park.

LEVAIN BAKERY:

167 W 74th Street, New York, NY 10023 or 351 Amsterdam Ave, New York, NY 10024

WHOLE FOODS:

10 Columbus Circle Ste Sc101, Floor B1, New York, NY 10019

♥ Belvedere Castle, Central Park

LITTLE ISLAND

Little Island at Pier 55 is one of Manhattan's newest outdoor spaces, having only opened in May 2021. It's located in Hudson River Park, so it boasts wonderful views across the Hudson River to New Jersey, as well as all the way downtown to One World Trade Center.

During the summer months, there are dozens of events, shows, and performances at Little Island, and other occasions such as comedy shows, bingo, sing-alongs, and more.

If you're after a chilled-out date in the park, grab some snacks from Chelsea Market—try doughnuts from Doughnuttery, a hot dog from Berlin Currywurst, or a hearty portion of beef noodle soup from Very Fresh

PRO TIP

Just a short walk from Little Island resides Pier 57 Rooftop Park, which is another awesome outdoor space to hang out in New York. Here you can enjoy even more views of the city's skyline, plus you'll get to see Little Island from a different perspective.

Having only opened in April 2022, it's been anointed as New York's newest and largest rooftop park, and with breathtaking views, gorgeous seating areas, and beautiful flowers, it's clear to see why it's already a popular date hotspot in the city.

Noodles—and enjoy eating and relaxing together in the sunshine.

Alternatively, you can enjoy some delicious treats from Union Square Events, located within Little Island itself at the Play Ground. Here you'll find food such as banh mi, lobster rolls, beef brisket, salads, wraps, and so much more. Food stalls from Union Square Events only operate from May until September.

♥ LITTLE ISLAND:

Hudson River Park, Pier 55, W 13th Street, New York, NY 10014

♥ DOUGHNUTTERY, BERLIN CURRYWURST & VERY FRESH NOODLES:

Chelsea Market, Main Concourse, 425 W 15th Street, New York, NY 10011

♥ PIER 57 ROOFTOP PARK:

57 Hudson River Greenway, New York, NY 10011

THE BATTERY

Formerly known as Battery Park, this 25-acre green space resides at the very southern tip of Manhattan, just a few blocks from the One World Trade Center and Wall Street. It's also the place where you'll find the ticketing kiosk for Statue City Cruises, which take you on a tour around the harbor to the Statue of Liberty and Ellis Island.

The Battery is arguably at its finest during the spring and summer months when the sunset looks magical across the harbor and the Hudson River. It's a great spot to spy the Statue of Liberty as well.

There are a few cafés and restaurants located within the Battery itself, including The View at The Battery, which serves a plethora of sandwiches, salads, burgers, pastas, tacos, and more, making it a perfect addition to a date in the park.

NOT TO MISS

From the Battery, it's just a short 15-minute walk along South Street to Pier 15, a two-story structure residing on the East River that affords spectacular views of the Brooklyn Bridge and skyline.

You can enhance your date by enjoying drinks at the Watermark, which serves fancy cocktails, a variety of beer, prosecco, and wine.

THE BATTERY:
New York, NY 10004

THE VIEW AT THE BATTERY:
1 Battery Pl, New York, NY 10004

WATERMARK:
78 South Street, Pier 15, New York, NY 10038

WASHINGTON SQUARE PARK

Washington Square Park is one of the most renowned parks in New York City, largely thanks to its defining arch that honors the park's namesake: George Washington. If you get the angle just right, you can see the Empire State Building through the arch, making it a gorgeous photo opportunity to commemorate your date.

At the very heart of the park resides a fountain, which is a popular meeting spot for locals, tourists, and daters alike. During the summer months, there are street performers and buskers who put on a spectacular show.

GRAB A BITE

On the south side of the park, check out NY Dosas for some of the best Indian take-away food in Manhattan. Roti and veg will cost you $9, whereas a samosa is only $3, making this the perfect stall to pick up some food to enjoy inside the park or on a leisurely stroll afterward.

Head to the park's chess tables if you fancy challenging your date's competitive side, or simply watch the experts play quick-round games of chess—the locals have been doing it for years.

While you're in Greenwich Village, check out the *Friends* apartment building and Carrie

Bradshaw's apartment, both of which are less than a 10-minute walk from Washington Square Park. *Friends* and *Sex and the City* are incredibly iconic New York-based TV shows that are famed for showing the dating lives of the main characters, so visiting these apartments on a date in NYC seems incredibly fitting.

WASHINGTON SQUARE PARK:

5 Avenue, Waverly Pl, W 4 Street and Macdougal Street, New York, NY 10012

NY DOSAS:

50 Washington Square S, New York, NY 10012

FRIENDS APARTMENT:

90 Bedford Street, New York, NY 10014

CARRIE BRADSHAW'S APARTMENT:

66 Perry Street, New York, NY 10014

BROOKLYN BRIDGE PARK

Brooklyn Bridge Park is an 85-acre urban oasis on the edge of the Hudson River, and it's undoubtedly one of the best outdoor spaces in Brooklyn. Brooklyn Bridge Park is completely free to visit, and with outstanding views of the Brooklyn Bridge and back across the river to Manhattan, it's a wonderful place to enjoy a date.

The park comprises six piers, with Pier 2 being home to the beloved Roller Rink (see page 152) and Pier 4 housing its very own beach. Squibb Park Bridge is where you'll find unparalleled views of the Manhattan skyline, making it a great place to snap a photo memento of your date.

There are so many great places to eat nearby, including the infamous Shake Shack, The Osprey, and PILOT—an upscale, floating oyster bar on Pier 6 that is an ideal eating spot if you're looking for a fancy lunch date. The

LOOKING FOR LUXURY

For a sumptuous date in Brooklyn Bridge Park, visit the tour operator NYC by Water to rent your own private luxury yacht for the afternoon. Prices start at $2,250 plus $300 for captain and crew and an additional $100 for fuel. It's definitely not cheap, but it will undoubtedly be one of the most lavish and extravagant dates you've ever had.

bar is housed on a vintage boat and serves opulent seafood dishes, elegant cocktails, and expensive wine.

If luxury food doesn't pique your interest, head to River Deli, which is just a short three-minute walk from Pier 5. Here you'll find Sardinian-inspired brunch dishes on a more affordable budget where you can eat inside the restaurant or take your food away to enjoy in the park. Choose from dishes such as bruschetta, spaghetti carbonara, lasagna, and salad.

In the summer, you can visit Movies with a View, where dozens of classic Hollywood films and new releases are showcased on the Harbor View Lawn in the park. Bonus, it's free!

BROOKLYN BRIDGE PARK:

334 Furman Street, Brooklyn, NY 11201

SHAKE SHACK:

1 Old Fulton Street, Brooklyn, NY 11201

THE OSPREY:

60 Furman Street, Brooklyn, NY 11201

PILOT:

Brooklyn Bridge Park, Pier 6, Brooklyn, NY 11201

RIVER DELI:

32 Joralemon Street, Brooklyn, NY 11201

MOVIES WITH A VIEW:

Brooklyn Bridge Park Greenway, Brooklyn, NY 11201

NYC BY WATER:

159 Bridge Park Drive, Brooklyn, NY 11201

LET'S GET A DRINK

New York is one of the most iconic cities in the world for its bars and nightlife scene, so planning a date to one of the city's rooftop bars or old-timey pubs is sure to be a winner.

230 FIFTH

Located just a few blocks from the Empire State Building, 230 Fifth rooftop bar is one of the city's largest indoor and outdoor rooftop event spaces, with more than 33,000 square feet of dancing, drinking, and eating space.

Head to the 20th floor for an indoor drinking and dining experience like no other. Completely enclosed, this rooftop space is ideal if you want to remain cozy inside while still enjoying an array of drinks, dishes, and desserts.

For some of the best views of the Empire State Building in the whole of New York City, venture up one more flight of stairs to the 21st floor where you'll be greeted by the most breathtaking rooftop view of Manhattan. From here, you can see all the way downtown to the One World Trade Center, as well as the surrounding towering

NOT TO MISS

If you're feeling extra special, book a table for bottomless brunch; prices start at $45 per person for unlimited cocktails, prosecco, or coffee, plus a choice of an entree such as chicken caesar salad, fish and chips, pancakes, french toast, and more. Table reservations for bottomless brunch last for 90 minutes, but you can then head to the outdoor rooftop as there is no limit to the amount of time that you can spend at 230 Fifth.

skyscrapers that house the observation decks at the Empire State Building (see page 16) and Summit One Vanderbilt (see page 20).

In the winter months, 230 Fifth transforms into a winter wonderland, complete with giant inflatable igloos, cozy cabins, and toasty fires that provide the perfect setting for a romantic date night.

If you're heading on a date in the summer, you'll be able to take refuge under the shade of the umbrellas and the mini palm trees while sipping a delightful daiquiri or a mouthwatering mojito.

 230 FIFTH:
230 5th Avenue, New York, NY 10001

TIME OUT MARKET NEW YORK

Comprising an impressive 24,000 square-foot waterfront dining complex, Time Out Market New York is a multi-level rooftop bar and food court that's home to a smorgasbord of some of New York's best eateries.

On the ground floor, you'll find Felice Pasta Bar, Ess-a-Bagel, and Pat LaFrieda Meat Purveyors, plus many more. Here you can enjoy your date inside the food court or head outside to the nearby Brooklyn Bridge Park for al fresco dining.

Head up to the fifth floor of Time Out Market New York, and you'll discover one of the best rooftop bars and terraces in the city. From here, you can marvel at the magical views of the Brooklyn Bridge, Manhattan Bridge, and the iconic New York skyline. Serving a plethora of classic cocktails as well as some of their very own signature cocktails—definitely try the Very Berry Sangria

NOT TO MISS

After you've enjoyed a tipple or two at the rooftop bar, head over the Brooklyn Bridge for a romantic stroll just in time for sunset. You'll be treated to spectacular golden-hour views of both the Manhattan and Brooklyn skylines.

and the Dumbo Drop—this rooftop bar is a fantastic place for a date.

Visit the market from 4:00 PM to 7:00 PM, Monday to Friday, to take advantage of happy hour where you can enjoy draught beer from $5, wine from $7, and cocktails from $8.

TIME OUT MARKET NEW YORK:

55 Water Street, Brooklyn, NY 11201

A.R.T. NOMAD (ARLO HOTEL)

Residing just on the edge of Koreatown, 31 stories above the ground, the Arlo Roof Top bar on top of the Arlo NoMad hotel is a wonderful place for a boozy date. With unparalleled views of the Empire State Building and the surrounding skyscrapers in the NoMad neighborhood, this brilliant rooftop bar is an enchanting setting in Midtown Manhattan.

Sip decadent cocktails, dunk tasty homemade pita bread into an array of dips, and relax and unwind in the comfy outdoor furniture. Check out the rooftop's infamous glass floor installation that boasts plunging views all the way down to the streets of Manhattan below.

Reservations aren't always required, but it's usually best to book a table for the rooftop bar in advance to avoid disappointment, especially in the busy summer months.

PRO TIP

Madison Square Park is just five blocks south of the Arlo Hotel, which provides the perfect place for an after-dinner stroll. Be sure to check out the Flatiron Building while you're there, as it's a great photo opportunity to commemorate your date.

Once you've soaked up the rooftop views, head back down to the first floor of the Arlo NoMad Hotel to its signature Middle East-inspired restaurant, Lamalo. Here you can indulge in a Middle East feast of lamb kofta, shakshuka, tahini, and more.

A.R.T. NOMAD:

Arlo Hotel NoMad, 11 E 31st Street, Rooftop, New York, NY 10016

MCSORLEY'S OLD ALE HOUSE

Dating all the way back to 1854, McSorley's Old Ale House is the oldest Irish bar in the whole of New York City. Specializing in just two different types of ale—light and dark—McSorley's is an iconic institution in the heart of New York that cannot be missed. With sawdust-strewn floors, archaic decorum, vintage posters plastered on the walls, and locals who've been frequenting this enigmatic joint for generations, McSorley's Old Ale House is sure to be a unique date.

PRO TIP

Located in the East Village, McSorley's is in a prime location for visiting some of New York's other top food and drink establishments, so if you're in the mood for a bit of a bar crawl, make sure you tag the likes of The Library, Doc Holliday's, and Beetle House onto your visit to McSorley's Old Ale House.

Order one beer and you'll be served two glasses; order a cocktail and you'll be laughed out of there. It's certainly a no-frills approach bar, but its distinctive charm is hard to dismiss. It's also a cash-only establishment, which is a rarity when it comes to drinking at a bar in New York, but this only adds to its creative charm.

History oozes through the walls, and whether you grab a standing position at the bar or a seat at one of the huge, communal tables, you can guarantee that your time at McSorley's will be a memorable occasion.

MCSORLEY'S OLD ALE HOUSE:

15 E 7th Street, New York, NY 10003

THE LIBRARY:

7 Avenue A, New York, NY 10009

DOC HOLLIDAY'S:

141 Avenue A, New York, NY 10009

BEETLE HOUSE:

308 E 6th Street, New York, NY 10003

PANORAMA ROOM

Boasting impressive 360-degree views of New York City, the Panorama Room rooftop bar is situated at the top of the Graduate Roosevelt Island Hotel. With its exclusive location in the middle of the East River on Roosevelt Island, you'd be hard-pressed to find a more unique rooftop bar in the city.

While Roosevelt Island itself might not be much to look at, the views from the Panorama Room's 18th-floor outdoor terrace offers spectacular sights of the Ed Koch Queensboro Bridge, and you can also see the iconic Chrysler Building, the Freedom Tower, and the Empire State Building.

A luxury brunch menu of East Coast oysters and a sea-food tower await your arrival at the Panorama Room, complete with premium cocktails such as the Duke of New York, a White Negroni, or The Looking Glass.

At the indoor oval-shaped bar, you'll be treated to sumptuous cocktail creations. On the outdoor terrace, sounds of maritime traffic provide a soothing back-ground buzz as a gentle breeze from the East River cloaks the rooftop.

Reservations aren't essential to visit the Panorama Room, but it's worth reserving a spot in advance to avoid disappointment, especially as it only opened at the

end of 2021. It's set to become one of the city's ultimate rooftop hotspots.

♥ THE PANORAMA ROOM:
22 N Loop Road, New York, NY 10044

FOODIE HOTSPOTS

If you're looking for a good date spot in New York City that comprises excellent food, a wonderful ambience, and impeccable service, take a look at the five best dining experiences in New York.

BRUNCH CRUISE

A brunch cruise around Manhattan is undoubtedly one of the most romantic dining experiences you can enjoy in the city. Classic Harbor Line offers dozens of cruises around Manhattan, and their Around Manhattan Brunch Cruise is one of the best brunch options in New York. Lasting almost three hours and costing $124 for four or more adults or $142 for two to three adults, this magnificent tour takes you on a full circumnavigation of the island of Manhattan, passing underneath 20 bridges as you slowly sail around the island's coast.

On board a choice of two 1920s luxury yachts, you can indulge in a prestigious three-course menu consisting of classic New York bagels, homemade quiches, salads, salmon, pastries, fresh fruit, and more. Brunch is served with a complimentary drink of your choice.

An alternative brunch cruise provider in Manhattan is the Bateaux New York, provided by City Experiences by Hornblower. This lavish, luxury brunch cruise offers spectacular views of both the East and Hudson Rivers as you gently sail around the island.

This cruise lasts for approximately two and a half hours. Paired with bottomless mimosas and a hearty plate of food, you'll enjoy DJ entertainment and a glorious backdrop of the Manhattan skyline. The Bateaux New

York brunch cruise costs $115 per adult or $147 for a guaranteed window seat.

♥ AROUND MANHATTAN BRUNCH CRUISE:
Chelsea Piers, Pier 62, W 22nd Street, New York, NY 10011

♥ BATEAUX NEW YORK PREMIER BRUNCH CRUISE:
Chelsea Piers, Pier 61, W 23rd and 12th Avenue, New York, NY 10011

SELF-GUIDED PIZZA TOUR

Pizza is at the very heart of New York City's culinary scene, so a date where you explore the city's best pizza joints is sure to be a major success. With thousands of pizzerias spread across the five boroughs and an estimated 500,000 pizzas eaten every single day in NYC, it's no surprise that it's effortless to find somewhere to grab a slice. If you're planning a pizza tour for a date, you'll need to make sure that you hit the best spots.

Joe's Pizza has been a pizza institution in New York since 1975, when Joe Pozzuoli founded the iconic pizza landmark in Greenwich Village. Today, there are five locations of Joe's Pizza spread out across Manhattan and Brooklyn. With the most highly rated pizza joints on

PRO TIP

For some extra fun after you've tucked into a scrumptious slice from Prince Street Pizza, head a couple of blocks west to the Museum of Ice Cream for a sweet treat to cleanse your palate.

The Museum of Ice Cream makes for a perfect addition to your pizza-themed date, as it's a quirky and innovative immersive experience that allows you to rediscover your inner child. Learn about ice cream and its fascinating history through 13 multi-sensory installations and sample as many delicious desserts as you'd like before taking a ride on the highest indoor slide in New York City.

Broadway or Carmine Street, you'll never be too far from a slice.

If you visit the Broadway branch, take your slice to the nearby Bryant Park, where you can enjoy your cheesy masterpiece while people watching in the park. The Times Square 42nd Street subway station is also opposite the store, so you can hop on a train to another part of the city for your next round of pizza.

East Village Pizza is another hotspot that you should visit on your self-guided pizza tour of Manhattan, as their cheesy garlic knots are famous the world over and their vast range of pizza slices and whole pies are spectacular. Head here with a hearty appetite, especially if you want to try the garlic knots. They're a great portion size, making them perfect for sharing on a pizza-themed date in the city.

Prince Street Pizza is another iconic pizza location in Manhattan that's beloved by celebrities such as Kate Hudson, Rebel Wilson, Chris Hemsworth, and many more who cite it as the best pizza joint in the city. Expect long queues outside and no-frills service once you're inside.

JOE'S PIZZA:

7 Carmine Street, New York, NY 10014 and 1435 Broadway, New York, NY 10018

EAST VILLAGE PIZZA:

145 1st Avenue, New York, NY 10003

PRINCE STREET PIZZA:

27 Prince Street A, New York, NY 10012

MUSEUM OF ICE CREAM:

558 Broadway, New York, NY 10012

FLAME HIBACHI DOWNTOWN

For a more formal and intimate dining experience, head to Flame Hibachi Downtown. For this incredible Japanese culinary occasion, you can dine at a high table with the hibachi flame grill at the center. Their teppanyaki menu offers a choice of entrees served with one appetizer, hibachi vegetables, salad, and jasmine rice.

Opt for chicken, a vast variety of different cuts of steak, seafood such as swordfish, salmon, and shrimp, or a vegetarian alternative; pair it with the complimentary side dishes for one of the best Asian-inspired meals in the city.

Your food will be theatrically prepared for you on the hibachi grill table right in front of your eyes. While the food itself is exceptional, it's the cooking performance

PRO TIP

After your date, head to the observation deck at the Empire State Building, which is only a 15-minute walk from the downtown branch of Flame Hibachi. Alternatively, you can walk your dinner off with a stroll around Madison Square Park, which is less than 10 minutes away.

The Factory 380 is also just down the road on 3rd Avenue, and this lively Andy Warhol–themed haunt is the perfect place for a cocktail or digestif.

that will secure it as one of the most romantic dates in New York.

If the teppanyaki grill doesn't sate your appetite, visit Flame Hibachi at lunchtime and tuck into their wok and dim sum lunchtime specials. You can also enjoy the lunchtime hibachi special, which is slightly cheaper than the dinner alternative.

FLAME HIBACHI DOWNTOWN:
381 3rd Avenue, New York, NY 10016

EMPIRE STATE BUILDING:
20 W 34th Street, New York, NY 10001

MADISON SQUARE PARK:
11 Madison Avenue, New York, NY 10010

THE FACTORY 380:
380 3rd Avenue, New York, NY 10016

CHELSEA MARKET

Chelsea Market is renowned for being one of the best food halls in Manhattan, and thanks to its variety of food stalls and pop-ups, it makes for an excellent place to go on a food-inspired date in NYC.

Comprising a whopping 1.2 million square feet of event space and 40,500 square feet of food stalls alone, inside Chelsea Market you'll find an abundance of wonderful cuisines and beverages. It's a good idea to visit Chelsea Market with a roaring appetite so that you can do a mini food tour of the many vendors inside the market. For something rich and hearty, visit Berlin Currywurst for exquisite German sausages, Los Tacos No. 1 for divine Mexican cuisine, or Doughnuttery for the finest sugary doughnuts in the city.

PROMENADE ON THE HIGH LINE

Located in the Meatpacking District, Chelsea Market is just a stone's throw away from numerous entrance points for the High Line, so you can take advantage of the close proximity to this incredible outdoor space that's perfect for a romantic stroll in the summer.

Grab a bite to eat and then venture on the one-mile walk toward Hudson Yards to check out the quirky Vessel beehive structure for free.

Chelsea Market is also home to plenty of local stores and worldwide brands such as the Manhattan Fruit Market, Anthropologie, and Posman Books. Prolong your date by checking out the awesome shopping vendors. Perhaps you can even pick up something to commemorate your date.

CHELSEA MARKET:

75 9th Avenue, New York, NY 10011

VESSEL:

20 Hudson Yards, New York, NY 10001

BALTHAZAR

Opened in the spring of 1997 and listed in *Restaurant Magazine's* "World's 50 Best Restaurants," Keith McNally's Balthazar French brasserie in SoHo simply oozes elegance, luxe, and romance. This fine-dining experience provides an opulent date setting like no other.

An iconic French eatery whose dishes rival even those curated and cooked along the Seine, Balthazar is arguably New York City's most prestigious French restaurant and one that simply cannot be missed.

There are several menus to dig into at Balthazar: for an alternate dining experience, visit Balthazar for breakfast where you can indulge in dishes of eggs benedict, smoked salmon tartine, and egg-white omelets.

PRO TIP

After dinner, head to A.R.T. SoHo—which is A.R.T. NoMad's Lower Manhattan counterpart—where you can enjoy more cocktails on the rooftop with arresting views of the Freedom Tower and the Hudson River.

If you're dining at dinner time, you'll enjoy quintessential French cuisine such as steak frites, salade niçoise, bœuf bourguignon, and duck confit, finished with a dessert menu consisting of crème fraîche strawberry shortcake, crème brûlée, and profiteroles.

It's best to make a reservation ahead of time, especially if you're heading there for dinner, as tables get booked up weeks in advance and you don't want to miss out on this fantastic restaurant.

BALTHAZAR:
80 Spring Street, New York, NY 10012

A.R.T. SOHO:
231 Hudson Street, 11th Floor, New York, NY 10013

FREE
DATES

In a city as expensive as New York, it's always a revelation when you find something completely free to do. In this next section, you'll learn more about the city's finest, most romantic, and—most importantly—budget-friendly things to do.

STATEN ISLAND FERRY

The Staten Island Ferry is an esteemed establishment in New York City. It has been transporting locals back and forth between Manhattan and Staten Island for free since 1997.

Thankfully, it's not just the locals on both islands who get to take advantage of this incredible service. Tourists and date-goers alike are able to hop on the ferry and travel its route between Staten Island and Lower Manhattan.

In just one year, 22 million people frequent Upper Bay thanks to the Staten Island Ferry. With its departure point from the Battery, you'll be treated with views of some of New York's best sights, including Lady Liberty herself, the Freedom Tower, Ellis Island, Brooklyn Bridge, and more—completely free of charge.

A round trip without disembarkation isn't possible, but you can get off the ferry once it arrives at Staten Island and then rejoin the boarding queue to jump straight back on the return ferry again. Alternatively, stay on Staten Island for a while and explore North Shore Esplanade Park before grabbing an ice cream from the Häagen-Dazs store next to the pier just before you jump back on the ferry to Manhattan.

The ferry runs 24 hours a day, seven days a week. On weekdays, ferries depart from each terminal every 15

to 20 minutes during the busy rush hours, and every 30 minutes on weekends.

As the ferry is primarily used by commuters who live and work between the two islands, it gets tremendously crowded during the rush hours between 6:00 AM and 9:30 AM and 3:30 PM and 8:00 PM, so it's best to avoid a trip during those hours.

MANHATTAN TERMINAL:
4 Whitehall Street, New York, NY 10004

STATEN ISLAND TERMINAL:
1 Bay Street, Staten Island, NY 10301

HÄAGEN-DAZS:
Empire Outlets, Staten Island, NY 10301

BROOKLYN BRIDGE

As New York's most iconic bridge—and coincidentally one of the city's most famous landmarks—the Brooklyn Bridge has been used as a backdrop for many romantic scenes in films such as *Sex and the City* and *The Perfect Man*. This landmark first opened back in May 1883. With more than 140 years of remarkable history and romantic tales to tell, it's safe to say that its imposing presence plays the perfect role on any date in New York.

The walk across the entire length of the bridge is approximately 1.1 miles (1.8 kilometers) and takes roughly half an hour, depending on how many times you stop to admire the surrounding views (which you definitely should!).

From the bridge's incredible vantage point, you can see all the way into the heart of Manhattan, and even as far

GRAB A BITE

If you embark on the journey across the bridge from Manhattan, spend some time in City Hall Park and grab a coffee and sweet treat from The Wooly Daily coffee shop before you walk over.

If you're departing from Brooklyn, or you'd like something tasty once you've walked over the bridge and arrived in Brooklyn, visit Jacques Torres Chocolate shop in Dumbo for decadent desserts and goodies such as chocolate truffles, cookies, caramel treats, hot chocolate, and more.

as the Empire State Building and the Chrysler Building.
Up close and personal, the monumental Freedom Tower
creates an imposing presence, and the Manhattan Bridge
can be seen from one side of the bridge and the Statue of
Liberty from the other.

Once on the bridge, you'll be surrounded by other
romantics playing out their own love stories, but the
bridge's popularity shouldn't dissuade you from choosing
it as the host of your next date.

♥ BROOKLYN BRIDGE:
New York, NY 10038

♥ THE WOOLY DAILY:
11 Barclay Street, New York, NY 10007

♥ JACQUES TORRES CHOCOLATE DUMBO:
66 Water Street, Brooklyn, NY 11201

Brooklyn Bridge

THE HIGH LINE

The High Line resides on a former abandoned railway line and is one of the most reputable and sought-after outdoor spaces in New York City. It begins on Gansevoort Street on the edge of the Meatpacking District and ends on West 34th Street, just next to Hudson Yards, and covers a total distance of approximately 1.45 miles (2.33 kilometers).

The High Line only opened to the public in 2009, and the most recent renovations were only officially completed in 2019, so it's a relatively new outdoor space in the city compared to many of the other parks featured throughout this book.

With stunning views of the city, including its very own miniature observation deck that provides wonderful vistas of Edge and other surrounding skyscrapers, it's an incredibly romantic part of New York.

GRAB A BITE

If you want to incorporate food and drink into your date while walking along the High Line, you'll find plenty of eateries to sate your appetite. There's a Shake Shack branch at the beginning of the route on Gansevoort Street; L'Arte del Gelato on 15th Street, which serves up the tastiest gelato and sorbets; and Hearth on the High Line where you can enjoy delicious snacks that are perfect for sharing on a date.

Along the route, you'll find various park attractions: the Diller–von Furstenberg Sundeck & Water Feature; the Chelsea Market Passage, where you can hop back down to the street level below to check out the food and beverage stalls inside the market; and the Crossroads at 30th Street, which is the widest section of the High Line.

THE HIGH LINE:
Gansevoort Street to 34th Street, New York, NY 10011

SHAKE SHACK:
820 Washington Street, New York, NY 10014

L'ARTE DEL GELATO:
75 9th Avenue, New York, NY 10011

HEARTH ON THE HIGH LINE:
10th Avenue and W 15th Street, New York, NY 10011

TIMES SQUARE

The dazzling lights emanating from the enormous billboards, the street performers playing host to a world of different cartoon characters, and the abundance of alluring tourist shops make Times Square one of the most famous and beloved places in New York City.

Chocolate lovers need to visit M&M's World New York, which comprises a whopping 25,000 square feet of exclusive chocolate goodies across three floors. It's free to go inside and admire the multi-level chocolate shop, although you may feel inclined to purchase a treat or two as a souvenir.

Located in the small section known as Father Duffy Square, the iconic Red Steps of Times Square sit atop the TKTS booth, and they're the perfect place to people watch and admire the twinkling lights of the billboards and advertisements. If you spent all day at

SEASONAL ROMANCE

Just one block from Broadway in Times Square is the magnificent Bryant Park, which is a hub for date-goers all year round. In the winter, its spectacular Winter Holiday Market and ice skating rink provide the perfect backdrop for a cozy, festive date. In the summer, the open-air movie screen is a fantastic free activity to enjoy in the city.

this panoramic viewpoint, you'd likely see more than a million people contributing to the manic hustle and bustle of Times Square.

For an exclusive and lavish experience in Times Square, head to the St. Cloud Rooftop Bar at the Knickerbocker Hotel. From the 17th floor, you'll gain an incredible vista of the heart of Times Square below, and while the food and drink might cost a pretty penny, it's technically free to go up to the rooftop bar and admire the astonishing views below.

M&M'S WORLD TIMES SQUARE:
1600 Broadway, New York, NY 10019

TKTS BOOTH:
Broadway at W 47th Street, New York, NY 10036

ST. CLOUD ROOFTOP BAR:
6 Times Square, 17th Floor, New York, NY 10036

BRYANT PARK:
Between 40th and 42nd Street and 5th and 6th Avenue, New York, NY 10018

GRAND CENTRAL TERMINAL

Unquestionably, one of the most romantic locations in the city is Grand Central Terminal, thanks to the likes of *Friends with Benefits*, *Gossip Girl*, and *Before We Go* using it as a backdrop for both integral and charming scenes.

The architecture at this world-famous train station simply oozes romance and elegance, but it's also home to a fun and quirky attraction as well: the Whispering Gallery. This inconspicuous corner next to the Oyster Bar underneath the Main Concourse allows you to discreetly whisper into opposite corners of the archway.

More than 750,000 visitors frequent the echoing halls of Grand Central every single day, and while these numbers may be substantial, there are still plenty of hidden corners for you to enjoy a peaceful and romantic date.

GRAB A BITE

Once you've explored the majestic interiors, visit Grand Central Market to pick up some fresh produce from suppliers such as Eli's Bread and Murray's Cheese, and put together your very own picnic to enjoy in the nearby Bryant Park or inside the station's dining hall.

Access to Summit One Vanderbilt is also located within the grounds of Grand Central, so you can visit two of New York City's most sought-after landmarks all in one go.

GRAND CENTRAL TERMINAL:

89 E 42nd Street, New York, NY 10017

BRYANT PARK:

Between 40th and 42nd Street and 5th and 6th Avenue, New York, NY 10018

SPLASH-OUT DATES

Sometimes you just have to go big or go home when you really want to have a day to remember with that special someone. While this book largely contains epic date ideas that you can enjoy on a budget, this section details the best splash-out dates to enjoy in the city.

HELICOPTER RIDE

A helicopter ride over the Manhattan skyline is sure to be on many people's bucket lists, and it's an experience that you won't forget. HeliNY is one of the leading providers of helicopter tours in New York and New Jersey, and they have a range of helicopter tour packages to suit your budget.

Their New York Tour starts at $199 per person for a 12-to-15-minute ride over hotspots such as the Statue of Liberty, Central Park, and the Empire State Building. This is one of the cheapest helicopter tours in New York.

Their Deluxe Tour, on the other hand, costs $339 per person and lasts between 25 and 30 minutes. This tour covers a wider range of sights in the city and goes almost all the way to the northern tip of Manhattan Island.

FlyNYON is another helicopter tour provider that offers a vast range of options, including a doors-on and doors-off ride, a VIP tour, and a

AFTER TOUCHDOWN

If you're using HeliNY tour providers, enjoy a leisurely stroll through the Battery once you're safely back on the ground at the Downtown Manhattan Heliport. Head the 20-minute walk toward Brookfield Place where you can enjoy some shopping or indulge in a refreshing glass of wine at PJ Clarke's on the Hudson.

classic ride over New York City. Their prices range from $196 to over $1,500 per person on special occasions and holidays such as Thanksgiving and New Year's Eve. The FlyNYON tours depart from Kearny in New Jersey.

HELINY:
6 East River Piers, New York, NY 10004

FLYNYON:
78 John Miller Way, Kearny, NJ 07032

THE BATTERY:
New York, NY 10004

BROOKFIELD PLACE:
230 Vesey Street, New York, NY 10281

PJ CLARKE'S ON THE HUDSON:
250 Vesey Street, New York, NY 10281

♥ Manhattan skyline

LE BAIN & THE ROOFTOP AT THE STANDARD

New York City is home to a plethora of luxurious rooftop bars, but arguably none are as glamorous or prestigious as Le Bain at The Standard. From the breathtaking rooftop, enjoy exquisite views of Downtown Manhattan and the Freedom Tower. Thanks to The Standard's location along the High Line, you can also see the towering structure that houses the Edge observation deck.

Featuring performances from world-class DJs, opulent nibbles such as oysters, smoked salmon, and the High Line Platter, heavenly cocktail creations, and an out-of-this-world vantage point for sunset, Le Bain at The Standard simply screams extravagance and romance.

It's technically free to head to Le Bain and the rooftop, and even though it's not required to make a reservation before you go, it's a good idea to do so to avoid long queues. Keep in mind there are minimum spending requirements if you do make a reservation, which varies depending on the day and time of your visit.

You can also find the High Line Room & Terrace and The Top of The Standard located within the hotel itself. Despite being located on the third floor of The Standard Hotel, the High Line Room & Terrace still boasts dramatic

views of the High Line and the Hudson River from its elegant 3,100-square-foot covered terrace.

The Top of the Standard is the plush penthouse lounge that transforms into an exciting nightclub after 10:00 PM. If discos, dancing, and divine views are your and your date's speed, an evening at The Top of The Standard is sure to impress.

LE BAIN & THE ROOFTOP AT THE STANDARD:

The Standard, High Line, 848 Washington Street, New York, NY 10014

AFTERNOON TEA AT THE PLAZA

There are few hotels as famous as The Plaza in New York City. With movies such as *Home Alone 2: Lost in New York* and *Bride Wars* centering a huge chunk of their plot around this world-renowned landmark hotel, it's no wonder that it's so emblematic of love and romance.

Afternoon tea is served daily in The Palm Court inside The Plaza Hotel. It consists of a lengthy menu of both traditional afternoon tea treats and exclusive dishes and beverages, depending on your taste and budget.

LOOKING TO SPLURGE?

If you'd prefer to dine al fresco, The Plaza Hotel offers their very own "Perfect Plaza Picnic" package, in which expert staff set up a quintessentially romantic picnic in Central Park. The picnic menu comes with all the trimmings, from prosciutto with pear ginger jam to blue cheese sandwiches and a classic turkey breast with aged cheddar and dijon mayonnaise. For those with a sweet tooth, choose from a range of cookies, brownies, and caramels to create your very own dessert platter.

The Perfect Plaza Picnic package starts at $2,310 and is available if you book a stay at the hotel for a minimum of two nights in a Plaza King room or upward.

The Central Park Tea costs $118 per person and includes a vast range of sweet and savory delicacies such as freshly baked scones, lemon cheesecake, roast chicken sandwiches, and more. The Plaza Signature Tea costs $128 per person and includes a wider selection of desserts, pastries, and savory appetizers.

For a sumptuous afternoon tea at The Plaza Hotel, opt for the Grand Imperial Tea, which costs a whopping $599 for two people and is served with two glasses of fancy champagne and caviar.

If you want to enhance your date at The Plaza, a one-night stay in the cheapest room will set you back approximately $600, so it really is a once-in-a-lifetime extravagant experience.

 THE PLAZA:
5th Avenue, Central Park S, New York, NY 10019

BROADWAY SHOW

New York's Broadway is one of the most prestigious areas in the world of theater, and if you're looking to impress a date in NYC, a Broadway show is sure to wow with its razzle and dazzle.

The Lion King is the highest-grossing Broadway show of all time, amassing almost $2 billion since its inception in November 1997. The average ticket price is over $100, but some seats sell for well over $250, so it's easy to splash the cash when you're enjoying the entertainment provided by the on-stage lions, zebras, and hyenas.

Musicals such as *Hamilton*, *Chicago*, and *Dear Evan Hansen* are also among some of the highest-grossing and critically acclaimed Broadway shows of all time, and picking just one to watch for your date could prove to be a tricky task.

There are several ways to acquire tickets for a Broadway show, with one of the most popular methods being the TKTS booth located in the heart of Times Square. They provide on-the-day tickets with discounts up to 50 percent off, so it's definitely worth heading to the booth early in the day to see which shows have been discounted.

The most popular shows such as *The Lion King* and *Wicked* are not usually available via the TKTS booth, as they tend to sell out in advance, but you can sometimes get lucky and find a popular show with 20 to 50 percent off the initial ticket price.

You can also purchase tickets online in advance through the official broadway.com website, as well as through sites such as Ticketmaster and TodayTix. Additionally, you can buy them directly from the box office at each theater.

TKTS BOOTH:

Broadway at W 47th Street, New York, NY 10036

THE LION KING:

Minskoff Theater, 200 W 45th Street, New York, NY 10036

HAMILTON:

Richard Rodgers Theater, 226 W 46th Street, New York, NY 10036

CHICAGO:

219 W 49th Street, New York, NY 10019

DEAR EVAN HANSEN:

239 W 45th Street, New York, NY 10036

STAY AT THE MARK HOTEL

Home to more than 700 hotels, New York City isn't short of places to stay—so when it comes to choosing a lavish, romantic luxury hotel in New York, there's tough competition to find the very best one.

The Mark Hotel in Manhattan's desirable Upper West Side is often cited amongst professional hoteliers as one of the very best hotels in the city. Their most basic room comes with a price tag of around $1,000 a night, and a two-bedroom premier suite costs over $6,000 a night.

By the time you get to the three-bedroom suites, you can no longer book online, and instead, you have to call the hotel to discuss rates. It's no surprise, therefore, that The Mark Hotel is home to the most expensive hotel room in New York City and one of the most expensive hotel rooms in the entire world, with

NOT TO MISS

For the true epitome of romance, courtesy of The Mark Hotel, you can hire bicycles for the day and cycle down the beatific 5th Avenue and around Central Park.

For an additional cost at the discretion of the hotel, you can also arrange a perfectly assembled picnic prepared by world-class chef Jean-Georges Vongerichten.

The Mark Penthouse costing a stupendous $75,000 a night.

Adjacent to Central Park and boasting tremendous dining experiences, an on-site hair salon, a world-class fitness center, and treats by highly coveted patisserie aficionado Laudrée, a stay at this 5-star establishment is one to remember.

 THE MARK HOTEL:
25 E 77th Street, New York, NY 10075

SUMMER
FUN

Summer in New York is when the city really comes alive. With outdoor cinemas, music festivals, sunset views on rooftop bars, and a plethora of many more sun-based activities, there's nothing quite like a date in New York City during the summer.

CONEY ISLAND

Located in southwestern Brooklyn, Coney Island is an entertainment area and funfair complex located within its very own peninsular neighborhood. Home to over 50 rides and attractions, Coney Island is usually synonymous with family fun during the summer months in New York City, but it's also a fantastic place to enjoy a date in the lovely weather.

Coney Island is often cited as the birthplace of the hot dog in New York, and Nathan's Famous Hot Dogs has been an institution on the island since 1916, with their world-renowned hot dog eating competition taking place yearly since the 1970s. If guzzling dozens of sausages in record time doesn't take your interest, head to Luna Park for the best rides and attractions in the neighborhood. Whiz at full speed on the Coney Island Cyclone or try your hand at archaic and beloved arcade games such as whac-a-mole and ring toss.

To add a touch of romance, head to Al Cavallino Pizzeria for authentic Italian food, or share a substantial portion of mint chocolate chip or raspberry sorbet gelato from Coney's Cones.

You can buy wristbands at Luna Park, which allows you to spend four hours in the theme park and enjoy as many rides and attractions as you can during that time. Alternatively, you can opt for the pay-per-ride option,

which is available to purchase on the day of your visit.

Ride Deno's Wonder Wheel for a spectacular vantage point of the beach and surrounding amusement park before taking a stroll along Coney Island Beach. Boasting three sprawling miles of glorious sand, a vintage boardwalk, and plenty of other attractions along the way, Coney Island Beach is a must during the summer.

LUNA PARK AT CONEY ISLAND:
1000 Surf Avenue, Brooklyn, NY 11224

CONEY'S CONES:
1023 Boardwalk W, Brooklyn, NY 11224

DENO'S WONDER WHEEL:
3059 W 12th Street, Brooklyn, NY 11224

HIRE A BOAT FROM LOEB BOATHOUSE

Central Park boasts a wealth of incredible date opportunities, and an afternoon at the Loeb Boathouse is undoubtedly one of the best experiences in the vast 843 acres of the park.

From April to November, 10:00 AM to dusk, you can hire boats from the Loeb Boathouse to row around the Lake in the heart of Central Park. Boat hires cost $20 per hour and $5 for each additional 15 minutes. You can pay in cash, and you must also provide a $20 cash deposit.

If you'd prefer to let someone else do the hard work for you and you want to take a leaf out of Venice's romantic book, opt for an expertly captained gondola ride around the Lake instead. Gondola rides cost $50 per half an hour, and you should endeavor to reserve them in advance, as they're very

GRAB A BITE

Once you've rowed your way around the majestic water and admired the surrounding skyscraper cityscape, head inside the boathouse itself or to the outdoor bar for lunch. The restaurant at the Loeb Boathouse beautifully marries fine dining with a relaxed and intimate atmosphere, complete with unparalleled views of Central Park as you eat.

popular amongst date-goers in the summer.

Afterward, head to Bow Bridge, which is often cited as one of the most romantic spots in the whole city. It's where many engagements and wedding photoshoots take place, and thanks to its grandiose architecture and breathtaking views, it's clear to see why.

LOEB BOATHOUSE:
Park Drive North, E 72nd Street, New York, NY 10021

BOW BRIDGE:
Central Park, Bow Bridge, New York, NY 10024

MOVIE THEATER IN BRYANT PARK

From June to August, Bryant Park plays host to free outdoor movie nights every Monday evening. Each week, a different movie plays on a giant communal screen in the middle of the park, and famous films such as *Grease, The Godfather, Hairspray*, and *Indiana Jones* have all won spots on the big screen. This would be an incredible paid-for attraction, but the fact that it's free makes it an even more attractive date idea.

The movies don't usually start until around 8:00 PM, but the lawn opens between 4:00 PM and 5:00 PM so you can reserve a good spot. All large bags, backpacks, tables, and chairs are prohibited on the lawn, but you can bring a blanket to sit on for the duration of the movie.

Enjoy picnic treats and refreshing beverages from the on-site vendors inside the park from 4:00 PM and throughout the duration of the movie. The food and beverage retailers usually differ each year—vendors such as Hester Street Fair and Stout NYC have had the honors of partnering with Bryant Park in the past.

If picnic food doesn't interest you, head across the road on 43rd Street to STK Steakhouse Midtown before or after the movie for an award-winning meal and cozy lounge vibes.

♥ BRYANT PARK:
Between 40th and 42nd Street and 5th and 6th Avenue, New York, NY 10018

♥ STK STEAKHOUSE MIDTOWN:
1114 6th Avenue, New York, NY 10036

PIER 17 & SEAPORT

Located within the Seaport neighborhood just minutes from the Financial District is Pier 17, a diverse and immersive cultural hub during the summer months. Showcasing a range of concerts and performances from world-class artists, comedy events, and a variety of other exciting occasions, Pier 17's fantastic location and brilliant rooftop events space is the place to be.

From The Rooftop, you're treated to tremendous views of the East River as well as the Brooklyn skyline and bridge. Throughout the summer, you'll find huge stars such as Jason Mraz, Franz Ferdinand, and Blondie performing, all with epic views in the background.

If concerts aren't your thing, you might prefer the drinking and dining options at The Greens on the rooftop of Pier 17. Boasting mini lawns, a restaurant and bar area, and even a dedicated Patrón tequila patio area, there are plenty of places to grab a bite to eat and drink. Dive into giant s'mores, freshly prepared salads, fried chicken, burgers, ribs, and more and wash it all down with fancy cocktails and frozen refreshments.

A mere two-minute walk from Pier 17 takes you to the historic Seaport District where you can enjoy a plethora of different eateries, pop-up events, bookstores, vintage clothes shops, and so much more.

The newly opened Tin Building by Jean-Georges only arrived at the Seaport in the summer of 2022, and this fantastic creation combines food, retail, sounds, sights, and aromas all under one tin roof. The culinary scene is headed by critically acclaimed chef Jean-Georges Vongerichten, and there are more than 53,000 square feet of space to explore and enjoy.

PIER 17:

89 South Street, New York, NY 10038

TIN BUILDING:

96 South Street, New York, NY 10038

SUNSET AT BROOKFIELD PLACE

You'll find Brookfield Place just 100 yards from the One World Trade Center and Ground Zero Memorial, and this towering waterfront office and shopping complex has plenty of things to appreciate.

NOT TO MISS

Located directly on the waterfront and adjacent to Brookfield Place is Rockefeller Park, which comprises a vast area of immaculate lawns, gorgeous gardens, beautiful public art creations, and stunning scenes of the neighboring skyscrapers.

On a summer day, it's a romantic spot to grab some picnic grub from Battery Place Market and find somewhere peaceful and quiet to watch the sunset.

PJ Clarke's On The Hudson is a notable bar right on the Hudson River that offers remarkable sunset views, as well as a fanciful selection of wine, beer, spirits, and cocktails. From here, you can see over to the New Jersey skyline and even as far as the Statue of Liberty, which makes it one of the very best and somewhat secret sunset spots in the whole city.

Inside Brookfield Place shopping center, you'll find dozens of designer stores. Alternatively, head to the Loopy Doopy Rooftop Bar

for food, drink, and an even better view over the Hudson River.

BROOKFIELD PLACE:
230 Vesey Street, New York, NY 10281

PJ CLARKE'S ON THE HUDSON:
250 Vesey Street, New York, NY 10281

LOOPY DOOPY ROOFTOP BAR:
102 North End Avenue, New York, NY 10282

ROCKEFELLER PARK:
75 Battery Place, New York, NY 10280

BATTERY PLACE MARKET:
240 Murray Street, New York, NY 10282

WINTER ROMANCE

New York in winter is undoubtedly one of the most magical times you'll ever experience. The twinkling lights of the Rockefeller Tree will make you feel like you've stepped onto the set of a Hallmark Christmas movie, and the snow-capped trees of Central Park feel like a whimsical wonderland. There's romance in the city year round, but arguably more so during the festive season; it really is an occasion like no other.

ICE SKATING AT WOLLMAN RINK

There are many brilliant places to go ice skating in the winter in New York, including Bryant Park, the Rockefeller Center, Brookfield Place, Chelsea Piers, and more—but arguably the best and most famous ice skating rink in the city finds its home in Central Park at the Wollman Rink.

Wollman Rink first opened in 1949 and has since welcomed millions of native New Yorkers and visitors to the ice to whiz around the rink with the city's monumental skyscrapers as its backdrop.

Wollman Rink usually opens in late October until early April, so there's plenty of time to hit the ice and bust out your best moves. Ticket prices vary enormously depending on the time and day that you visit, with off-peak tickets costing just $15 for adults or $25 each during peak times. Holiday tickets cost $35 each. On top of the ticket price, you'll also have to hire skates at $10 if you don't have your own.

PRO TIP

Once you're chilled to the bone, head over to La Maison du Chocolat at the Shops at Columbus Circle for some heavenly chocolate delights. This Parisian-inspired chocolate shop boasts lavish treats of macarons, eclairs, truffles, ganaches, and more.

Two other ice skating rinks can also be found inside Central Park: one at the very northern tip of the park known as Lasker Rink, and when incredibly cold and icy conditions permit, a free ice skating rink on Conservatory Water in the natural body of water. The ice must be consistently six inches thick to skate here, and you must bring your own skates.

WOLLMAN RINK:

830 5th Avenue, New York, NY 10065

LASKER RINK:

110 Lenox Avenue, New York, NY 10029

CONSERVATORY WATER:

E 72nd Street, New York, NY 10021

LA MAISON DU CHOCOLAT:

The Shops, 1st Floor, 10 Columbus Cir, New York, 10019

♥ Bow Bridge, Central Park

DYKER HEIGHTS LIGHTS

New York isn't a city to shy away from extravagant Christmas decorations. You'll find many amazing holiday displays in and around Manhattan, but arguably none will be as extreme as the Christmas lights found in the Brooklyn neighborhood of Dyker Heights.

The elaborate Dyker Heights Christmas Lights can be found on most homes between 11th and 13th Avenue and between 83rd and 86th Street, but many homes as far down as 77th Street also take part in the yearly decorating tradition.

The Christmas pageantry of decorating the whole neighborhood started decades ago, and every year since, more and more people adorn their houses with spectacular lights, ornate decorations, and house-sized inflatables.

PRO TIP

As Dyker Heights is a residential area with only a handful of places to eat, head back toward Dumbo and visit Juliana's for one of the best pizzas in the neighborhood.

Many houses begin the decorating process the day after Thanksgiving and leave the decorations up until New Year's Day, so there's plenty of time to visit the neighborhood and catch a glimpse of this marvelous, festive tradition.

The only downside is that Dyker Heights is far away from the

rest of the festivities and holiday displays in Manhattan and Brooklyn. If you're traveling from the heart of Manhattan, it would take you over 4 hours to walk, over half an hour to drive, or almost an hour and a half via multiple different subway lines to get there. But once you're there, it's a magical experience and one that's worth savoring.

DYKER HEIGHTS:

Between 83rd and 86th Street and 11th and 13th Avenue, Brooklyn, NY 11228

JULIANA'S:

19 Old Fulton Street, Brooklyn, NY 11201

BRYANT PARK HOLIDAY MARKET

There are a wealth of fun things to do at Bryant Park in the summer, but this little urban oasis is also a fantastic place to visit in winter thanks to the Bank of America Winter Village.

Every year, dozens of festive-themed market stalls descend on Bryant Park to offer visitors a plethora of gift ideas, souvenirs, festive baubles, delicious holiday treats and drinks, and much more. Vendors such as Doughnuttery and Crepe Café are on hand to provide mouthwatering delicacies, and gift stalls such as Infinity Lights and JustStars produce the most beautiful trinkets and treasures.

There's also the Bank of America 17,000-square-foot ice skating rink, which is technically the only free admission rink in the

PRO TIP

Be sure to check out the New York Public Library main branch (also known as the Stephen A. Schwarzman Building) while you're at Bryant Park. The library is home to some of the most romantic collections of stories in the world. Wander through the main halls or head to the Rose Main Reading Room for a bit of peace and quiet away from the hubbub of the city.

city—though you do have to pay to rent your skates if you don't have your own. Prices for skate rentals change on a daily and hourly basis, depending on how busy the rink is, so check online before you go.

The rink sits in the heart of the park surrounded by cozy cabins that serve warm drinks and scrumptious snacks. If you're not into skating, it's the perfect place to grab a beverage and watch others zoom around the rink.

BRYANT PARK:

Between 40th and 42nd Street and 5th and 6th Avenue, New York, NY 10018

NEW YORK PUBLIC LIBRARY:

476 5th Avenue, New York, NY 10018

ROCKEFELLER CENTER CHRISTMAS TREE

The Rockefeller Center Christmas tree might just be one of the most emblematic parts of New York at Christmas. With a history spanning more than nine decades, the Rockefeller Center Christmas tree is a beacon of light, joy, and festivity. Each year, it welcomes millions of visitors and admirers. Adorned with more than 50,000 twinkling lights, as well as a giant star that weighs hundreds of pounds, the Rockefeller Tree is the largest Christmas tree in New York every single year.

The annual tree-lighting ceremony is usually held in the first week of December, and its imposing presence usually remains at the Rockefeller Center until mid-January. It is lit from 6:00 AM to 12:00 AM daily and for 24 hours on Christmas Day. Underneath the dazzling lights resides the

GRAB A BITE

Inside the Rockefeller Center itself, there are dozens of incredible places to eat once you've worked up an appetite from skating or if you need a warm respite from the cold. Visit Fuku at rink level, an exquisite fried chicken joint from world-renowned chef David Chang, or stop by Black Seed Bagels for artisanal New York-style bagels.

ever-so-romantic Rockefeller Center ice skating rink. The rink officially opened on Christmas Day in 1936 and is now the height of Christmas in New York for visitors from near and far.

The famous sweets-and-toys shop FAO Schwarz is located within the Rockefeller Center complex. It's the perfect place to act like a big kid again and admire all the giant stuffed animals, the awesome selection of candy, and the fantastic giant LEGO® creations.

ROCKEFELLER CHRISTMAS TREE & ICE RINK:

600 5th Avenue, Rockefeller Center, New York, NY 10020

FUKU:

30 Rockefeller Plaza, New York, NY 10111

BLACK SEED BAGELS:

30 Rockefeller Plaza, Concourse Level, New York, NY 10111

FAO SCHWARZ:

30 Rockefeller Plaza, New York, NY 10111

SAKS FIFTH AVENUE LIGHT SHOW

Just across the road from the Rockefeller Center, you'll find the gargantuan department store of Saks Fifth Avenue. Similarly to the annual Rockefeller Christmas tree, Saks Fifth Avenue also hosts its own festive extravaganza in the form of a remarkable holiday light show. Each year, hundreds of thousands of LED lights don the 5th Avenue–facing façade of the 10-story building to create a magical winter wonderland masterpiece, complete with festive music.

Accompanying the holiday light show are numerous window displays that are ornately decorated each year with a different theme to celebrate the season. The building is usually adorned with its festive display at the end of November. The light show runs approximately every 10 minutes around 4:30 PM to 11:30 PM each day, and each performance lasts around two to three minutes.

GRAB A BITE

Just around the corner from Saks, you'll find plenty of places to eat, including Casa Limone. Casa Limone is a highly rated Italian restaurant that offers a set lunch menu for $30 per person or a set dinner menu for $45 per person.

Saks's holiday window display might be one of the most famous in the city, but almost every store on 5th Avenue from East 49th to East 59th Street takes part in decorating their storefronts for the holiday season. Once you've enjoyed the festive light show at Saks, wander down 5th toward Central Park to check out the rest of the window displays. Some of the most notably decorated stores include Tiffany & Co., Louis Vuitton, and Cartier.

SAKS FIFTH AVENUE:

611 5th Ave, New York, NY 10022

TIFFANY & CO.:

6 E 57th Street, New York, NY 10022

LOUIS VUITTON:

611 5th Avenue, 1st Floor, New York, NY 10022

CARTIER:

653 5th Avenue, New York, NY 10022

CASA LIMONE:

20 E 49th Street, New York, NY 10017

RELAXING RENDEZVOUS

In a city that's home to nearly nine million people, you'd be forgiven for thinking that there are very few places to enjoy a relaxing activity. Thankfully, there are a few hidden gems around the city that boast the perfect opportunity to reconnect with your inner peace—and that special someone.

THE COUPLE SPA

While the Upper East Side might not be quite as chaotic and hectic as Midtown Manhattan, it's not exactly a quiet hub, either. But nestled within the Manhattan mayhem just a few blocks from one of the many 5th Avenue Central Park entrances is The Couple Spa—a tranquil haven of calmness and serenity away from the hustle and bustle of the city. Renowned for offering treatments that boast both romance and relaxation, The Couple Spa is perfect for a relaxing date.

Choose from exclusive packages such as the Couple's Aromatherapy treatment, or take the romance one step further and opt for the Couple's Royal Bath, complete with dreamy massages, restorative body scrub treatments, and the pinnacle of all luxury: chocolate and champagne.

You can choose between a 100-minute session or a three-hour session, and you can also fine-tune your individual treatments to suit your needs and preferences.

Their newly opened Rose Room is also the perfect place for couples looking to escape the hecticness of

PRO TIP

Once you're fully relaxed and replenished, head to Serena's Wine Bar just around the corner for a laid-back atmosphere with delicious Italian nibbles and wine.

the city. It resides within its own private complex in the spa and offers visitors the chance to create their own Rose Room package, complete with treatments of their choice. There's also a fully stocked fridge of refreshing champagne, plus numerous other treats and goodies to compliment your ultimate spa experience.

♥ THE COUPLE SPA:
320 E 65th Street, New York, NY 10065

♥ SERENA'S WINE BAR:
1268 2nd Avenue, New York, NY 10065

BROOKLYN BOTANIC GARDEN

Encompassing 52 acres of gorgeous greenery in the heart of Brooklyn, the magnificent Brooklyn Botanic Garden is a tranquil oasis amidst the chaos of the city.

The Botanic Garden was originally founded more than 100 years ago, and over the years it has been transformed into a beautiful sanctuary. It's home to more than 12,000 different species of flora, with stunning collections of cherry blossoms, fruit trees, exotic plants, delicate roses, and a glorious avenue of magnolia.

GRAB A BITE

Overlooking the Lily Pool Terrace, the Yellow Magnolia Café is located on the eastern edge of the gardens and provides a wonderful weekday menu with dishes such as a garden mezze, healthy salads, hearty soups, and much more, all created with locally sourced ingredients.

The Rose Garden, Bonsai Museum, and the Water Garden are some of the most romantic spots in the Brooklyn Botanic Garden where you can enjoy peaceful strolls through the flourishing greenery.

Entrance to Brooklyn Botanic Garden is provided on a ticketed basis, and it costs $18 per adult to visit. Once you're

inside the gardens, you can spend hours relaxing in the grounds and exploring the thousands of species of plant life.

The Brooklyn Botanic Garden is located adjacent to Prospect Park and the Zoo, so once you've had a quiet wander around the gardens, head across Flatbush Avenue for the many walking routes, ponds, and lakes inside the larger park.

♥ BROOKLYN BOTANIC GARDEN:
990 Washington Avenue, Brooklyn, NY 11225

♥ Brooklyn Botanic Garden

AIRE ANCIENT BATHS

Another luxurious spa in New York, this time in Lower Manhattan, AIRE Ancient Baths are housed in the most beautiful historic industrial building that dates all the way back to 1808.

A journey of pure relaxation awaits once you step inside this establishment, with ancient thermal baths, massages, and spa treatments that will leave you feeling marvelous. There are also signature couples' packages that are best enjoyed together.

The soothing couples' massage is two hours and includes a wine bath that allows you to immerse yourself in an antioxidant-rich bath filled with Spanish Ribera del Duero red grapes—an unforgettable experience.

If being submerged in wine doesn't quench your thirst, try out one of the signature ancient offerings such as the Ultimate Bath Experience or the Himalayan Salt Experience, in which you'll be treated to 80 minutes of pure bliss in the form of a deep body scrub and rejuvenating massage.

PRO TIP

A 10-minute walk will take you to the west of the island where you can enjoy a leisurely stroll around Pier 26. Or, if you feel like injecting a bit of fun and adventure into your relaxing day, visit the mini golf course on Pier 25.

Afterward, explore the neighborhood's many local art galleries such as the Klaus von Nichtssagend Gallery and the Kerry Schuss Gallery for a look at their remarkable contemporary creations.

AIRE ANCIENT BATHS:
88 Franklin Street, New York, NY 10013

KLAUS VON NICHTSSAGEND GALLERY:
87 Franklin Street, New York, NY 10013

KERRY SCHUSS GALLERY:
73 Leonard Street, New York, NY 10013

PIER 26 AT HUDSON RIVER PARK:
Hudson River Greenway, New York, NY 10013

PIER 25 AT HUDSON RIVER PARK:
West Street, New York, NY 10013

PROSPECT PARK

Just a stone's throw from Brooklyn Botanic Garden is Prospect Park, home to its very own zoo, a gorgeous boating lake, stunning lookout points, and more.

Before you head inside the park, pay a visit to Overgreens Salads & Juice and pick up some delicious healthy salads, sandwiches, paninis, or omelets for a picnic lunch. The Bandshell Picnic Tables provide a wonderful place to pitch a picnic and devour your goods.

Hiring a pedal boat or kayak from the LeFrak Center at Lakeside is one of the most delightful and relaxing activities that you can enjoy in Prospect Park. A double pedal boat costs $44 for two people for one hour, and a double kayak costs $32 per hour.

You can also hire bicycles for as little as $16 each for an hour from the LeFrak Center, which makes for a romantic date as you meander your way through the 526 acres of Prospect Park.

The LeFrak Center also showcases seasonal ice and roller-skating opportunities, which tend to get a little crowded during the peak summer and winter months. If you visit on a weekday during the off season, you'll likely find it to be much quieter.

At the northern end of Prospect Park, you'll find Meadowport Arch and Endale Arch, which resemble the ones found in Central Park. They provide the perfect backdrop for a photo opportunity to commemorate your date experience.

OVERGREENS SALADS & JUICE:

193 Prospect Park W, Brooklyn, NY 11215

BANDSHELL PICNIC TABLES:

48-USA, 58 Prospect Park W, Brooklyn, NY 11215

LEFRAK CENTER AT LAKESIDE:

171 East Drive, Brooklyn, NY 11225

MEADOWPORT ARCH:

West Drive, Brooklyn, NY 11215

ENDALE ARCH:

Prospect Park, 11 East Drive, Brooklyn, NY 11215

Grand Army Plaza, entrance of Prospect Park

THE UNION·1861·1865

MOMA

The Museum of Modern Art, or MoMA as it's more commonly known, is one of the most renowned and beloved museums in the world. Located on 53rd Street between 5th and 6th Avenue, it's just a few blocks away from the Rockefeller Center in one direction and Central Park in the other, so this cultural art hub really is at the epicenter of the city's most prized attractions.

The MoMA is an eccentric art museum with almost 200,000 works of both modern and contemporary art in its collections. There's a continuous rotation of exhibits and collections on display, which gives you the opportunity to find a collection that speaks to you.

While the museum doesn't necessarily operate on a strictly silent basis, it's certainly much quieter and more peaceful than the likes of the American Museum of Natural History or the Met, making it a lovely place for a date if you want a space away from the commotion of the city.

Entrance to the museum costs $25 per adult, and you can spend as many hours as you

GRAB A BITE

For lunch, head to the fourth floor of the museum for a bite to eat at the Terrace Café. Find a quiet spot in the corner or on the outdoor terrace for views of the surrounding skyscrapers.

desire amongst its vast artwork collection during open-
ing hours.

MOMA:
11 W 53rd Street, New York, NY 10019

THE TERRACE CAFÉ:
11 W 53rd Street, 4th Floor, New York, NY 10019

EXCITING OUTINGS

It's fair to say that every single date idea listed throughout this book is fun and exciting, but in this section, you'll find some of the most thrilling experiences that you can enjoy with your partner in New York City.

COMEDY SHOW

Greenwich Village is known as the epicenter of hip bars, cafés, and restaurants. Alongside playing host to many off-Broadway shows and jazz clubs, it's also a cultural center for comedy in New York.

The New York Comedy Club is one of the most renowned providers of hilarious entertainment in the city, and with locations in both Midtown and the East Village, there's always something amusing to watch. Illustrious comedians such as Rachel Wolfson, Kevin Dombrowski, Jason Salmon, and Tom Cassidy all take residency at the New York Comedy Club. With daily performances at both locations many times a day, you're sure to find a lineup that suits your comedic preferences.

The Comedy Cellar is often cited as the best comedy club in the whole of the United States, and a visit to one of its many Greenwich Village–based locations will let you be the judge of that statement.

GRAB A BITE

Thanks to Greenwich Village's vast and varied array of restaurants and bars, you won't struggle to find somewhere to eat before or after watching a comedy show. The Spaniard is one of the top-rated bars and gastropubs in the West Village, known for its myriad supply of strong booze and hundreds of bottles of whiskey.

A lesser-known comedy club is The Grisly Pear in Greenwich Village, which combines an eclectic bar with a small stage of comedians to provide a night of uproarious entertainment. You can usually secure last-minute tickets to watch a performance at The Grisly Pear, often for as little as $10 a ticket, so not only is it a super-fun activity to enjoy, but it's remarkably affordable too.

NEW YORK COMEDY CLUB MIDTOWN:
241 E 24th Street, New York, NY 10010

NEW YORK COMEDY CLUB EAST VILLAGE:
85 E 4th Street, New York, NY 10003

COMEDY CELLAR AT MACDOUGAL STREET:
117 MacDougal Street, New York, NY 10012

COMEDY CELLAR AT THE VILLAGE UNDERGROUND:
130 W 3rd Street, New York, NY 10012

THE GRISLY PEAR:
107 MacDougal Street, New York, NY 10012

THE SPANIARD:
190 W 4th Street, New York, NY 10014

BROOKLYN ESCAPE ROOM

If you want to go on a date that veers away from the standard, run-of-the-mill ideas, booking a session at the Brooklyn Escape Room is an absolute must. Situated just around the corner from the home of the Brooklyn Nets basketball team, this is a fast-paced, fun, and immersive experience to take part in.

Trapped in a spooky haunted house, your mission is to work as a team and figure out how to escape the eerie establishment. It's not an activity for the fainthearted, as there are plenty of twists and turns that will likely frighten you at every stage, but it is an incredible amount of fun and a unique experience in New York.

An hour in the escape room costs $80 for two players. You can play with up to eight people in the room for an additional cost if you want to rope in your other couple friends to scare them senseless.

To calm your nerves once you've managed to escape, venture around the corner to Insomnia Cookies, where you can reward your bravery with a feast of chocolate delights.

PRO TIP

If you happen to time your visit to the Brooklyn Escape Room on a Brooklyn Nets game day, you could always head over to the Barclays Center afterward to enjoy an expeditious game of basketball.

BROOKLYN ESCAPE ROOM:
594 Pacific Street, Brooklyn, NY 11217

INSOMNIA COOKIES:
32 5th Avenue, Brooklyn, NY 11217

BARCLAYS CENTER:
620 Atlantic Avenue, Brooklyn, NY 11217

GAME AT MADISON SQUARE GARDEN

Madison Square Garden is one of the most famous sporting and performance venues in the world. Home of the legendary New York Knicks basketball team and the New York Rangers ice hockey team, this world-renowned arena is the perfect place to catch a game of some of America's most notable sports teams.

The average ticket price to watch a Knicks game at MSG is around $200 per person, so it's certainly not a cheap date in the city. One way to combat this extortionate ticket price but still watch a game at the arena is by securing tickets to a college basketball game. They usually only cost around $10 to $20 per person, making it a much more affordable option.

Both the basketball and ice hockey seasons usually run from October to April. For the rest of the year, you can expect to see some of the most celebrated artists and performers in the world take to the stage at MSG. Legendary artists such as Elvis Presley, Elton John, John Lennon, Madonna, Taylor Swift, Bruce Springsteen, and many others have performed in the highly coveted arena over the years. With dazzling lineups constantly on the horizon, you'll likely catch a performance of a lifetime if you time your date at Madison Square Garden right.

Located a couple of blocks east of the Garden is Candytopia, a sensational and immersive museum experience with colossal candy constructions. On top of admiring all of these marvelous creations, you'll also get to sample a ton of candy, which will leave you feeling like a kid in a sweet shop.

MADISON SQUARE GARDEN:
4 Pennsylvania Plaza, New York, NY 10001

CANDYTOPIA:
111 W 32nd Street, New York, NY 10001

PIER 2 ROLLER RINK

Earlier chapters equipped you with plenty of recommendations for the best ice skating rinks in New York City; now it's time to find the best roller skating rink. Pier 2 Roller Rink is often awarded this title thanks to its awesome location within Brooklyn Bridge Park and its surrounding city skyline views.

Regardless of whether you're a pro or an amateur skater, the Roller Rink at Pier 2 caters to abilities of all levels, making it tremendously fun even if you're terrible at the sport. The rink is technically outdoors, although there is a makeshift roof that provides some shelter during less desirable weather conditions.

Admission costs $7 per person and an additional $7 for skate hire if you don't have your own.

Once you've rolled your way around the rink, don't leave the pier quite yet, as it's the perfect opportunity to take a stroll around the promenade for exquisite views of the Manhattan

PRO TIP

If you're feeling particularly adventurous, visit Brooklyn Bridge Park Boathouse on a Wednesday, Thursday, or Saturday in the summer months to enjoy free kayaking sessions in the bay between Piers 1 and 2. Reservations are required and slots book up quickly, so be sure to reserve a spot well in advance to avoid disappointment.

skyline back over the East River. There aren't too many places to eat nearby, so you might want to head back toward Dumbo or even venture into Downtown Brooklyn, where you'll find a plethora of wonderful eateries to sate your appetite.

Park Plaza next to Cadman Park Plaza is a great spot if you want to grab a quick bite to eat; Gristedes is a fabulous little deli where you can pick up an assortment of premade lunch boxes, ranging from cheese and meat platters to hearty portions of noodles and spring rolls that make exemplary companions for enjoying a picnic in Cadman Park.

PIER 2 ROLLER RINK:

150 Furman Street, Pier 2, Brooklyn, NY 11201

BROOKLYN BRIDGE PARK BOATHOUSE:

10 Montague Street, Brooklyn, NY 11201

PARK PLAZA:

220 Cadman Plaza W, Brooklyn, NY 11201

CADMAN PARK PLAZA:

Cadman Plaza E, Brooklyn, NY 11201

GRISTEDES:

101 Clark Street, Brooklyn, NY 11201

ELLEN'S STARDUST DINER

Eating at Ellen's Stardust Diner is one of the most fun and quintessentially New York dining experiences you can have. The entertaining diner is a multi-level, fifties-themed hotspot where the waiters and waitresses are all aspiring Broadway performers. Their level of theatrical training and willingness to perform makes for a brilliant dining venture just off Times Square. Many of the waitstaff at Ellen's have actually gone on to be Broadway stars, so it's clear to see the immense level of talent you can expect while eating.

The food itself is also exceptional, and dishes such as fried chicken and waffles, Philly cheesesteak, and meatball subs will wow you with their substantial portions. You'll be serenaded while eating, which makes for a unique dining occasion, quite unlike some of the city's top-class luxury establishments.

Diners are encouraged to participate in the lighthearted production, and the staff love to put on a good show while singing Broadway classics. With retro decor and showbiz-themed memorabilia adorning the walls of the diner, Ellen's is a classic institute in the heart of New York.

Once you've stuffed your face and sang your heart out, head out into Times Square at night to catch a glimpse of the brightly lit billboards, or even grab a viewing of a

Broadway show immediately after to continue with the theatrical theme of the evening.

❤ ELLEN'S STARDUST DINER:

1650 Broadway, New York, NY 10019

ABOUT THE AUTHOR

Chloe Dickenson runs *Just A Girl*, an award-nominated UK travel blog that focuses on affordable luxury travel in the form of travel guides, accommodation recommendations, and restaurant reviews. She's worked with brands such as Babbel, Jet2, The TEFL Org, Aldi, Marks and Spencer, Visit Northumberland, The Great British Food Festival, Cosy Club, Hotels.com, Tinggly, Original Travel, Osprey, ghd, and many more. Dickenson writes for publications such as *Culture Trip*, *Bookaway*, *Rough Maps*, and *Trip101*, and her work has been featured in *BBC Business* and the *Yorkshire Press.*

ABOUT CIDER MILL PRESS BOOK PUBLISHERS

Good ideas ripen with time. From seed to harvest,
Cider Mill Press brings fine reading, information,
and entertainment together between the covers
of its creatively crafted books. Our Cider Mill
bears fruit twice a year, publishing a new
crop of titles each spring and fall.

"Where Good Books Are Ready for Press"

501 Nelson Place
Nashville, Tennessee 37214

cidermillpress.com